HELMSLEY CASTLE

NORTH YORKSHIRE

❖

Jonathan Clark D.Phil.

Set on a rocky outcrop overlooking the River Rye, the ruins of Helmsley Castle are impressive. The shattered remains of the east tower still dominate the town's skyline. Walter Espec had established the castle by the 1120s, providing a residence at the centre of his Yorkshire estates. Espec's castle was planned with two baileys, and enclosed by huge earthworks, which can still be seen today. Throughout the Middle Ages, the castle continued to evolve, with new buildings and more elaborate defences. This cycle of modernisation continued into the 16th century, when the medieval buildings were converted into a fine Tudor mansion, the remains of which can still be seen today. The conflict of the English Civil War resulted in the destruction of significant parts of the castle, but it continued in use as a residence until the early 18th century. Duncombe Park was being built at this time, its estate formed partly from the castle's medieval hunting parks and the lands of Rievaulx Abbey, and the castle became a Gothic ruin within its grounds. In the 19th and early 20th centuries, the castle was used, among other things, as a quarry, a tennis court and a chicken run. The current appearance of the castle owes much to Sir Charles Peers's restoration, after the site passed into State guardianship in 1923.

Above: A 13th-century carved head of a monk, excavated from the castle. It probably once decorated the chapel in the inner bailey

❖ CONTENTS ❖

Published by English Heritage
1 Waterhouse Square, 138-142 Holborn, London EC1N 2ST
© English Heritage 2004, reprinted 2006, 2008
Photographs by Bob Skingle, from the English Heritage Photographic Unit, and copyright of English Heritage, unless otherwise stated.

www.english-heritage.org.uk

FSC Mixed Sources
Product group from well-managed forests, controlled sources and recycled wood or fibre
www.fsc.org Cert no. SW-COC-002830
© 1996 Forest Stewardship Council

Commissioned and edited by Susannah Lawson
Print Production Elaine Pooke
Designed by Pauline Hull
Picture research by Diana Phillips
Diagrams by Richard Morris
Plan by Jonathan Clark
Reconstruction drawings by Peter Dunn and Philip Corke
Printed in England by Vitesse Printing Co
C40, 08/08, 05354, ISBN 978-1-85074-865-6

TOUR OF THE
CASTLE

❖

The tour starts at the Visitor Centre, and leads you round the castle as the medieval visitor might have experienced it. The plan on page 40 and the bird's-eye view on the previous page will help you to find your way round. As you leave the Visitor Centre, turn left and follow the path along the line of the outer ditch of the castle, which might have formed one of the medieval approaches to the castle.

THE CASTLE DITCHES

The ditches and ramparts, which surround the core of the castle, are one of the defining characteristics of the site. In origin they may predate Walter Espec's time, but they certainly formed an essential part of the castle that he established. The earth that was excavated from the ditches was used to construct the ramparts,

The castle from the west

❖ WALTER ESPEC ❖

Little is known of Walter Espec's life prior to his acquisition of Helmsley Castle in about 1120. Available evidence suggests that he might have been born in Bedfordshire, the son of a lesser Norman baron, William Spech, who is recorded at Warden in 1086. Walter was one of the foremost nobles in the north of England, enjoying considerable political success under King Stephen. He held the positions of Justiciar of the Forests and Justiciar of the Northern Counties from Henry I, and he led the English troops at the Battle of the Standard in 1138, fought near Northallerton in North Yorkshire. Espec gained significant amounts of land and wealth through these appointments, and he amassed large estates in both Northumberland and Yorkshire, centred on Wark and Helmsley respectively. Espec did not have any heirs to whom he could bequeath this wealth, and instead seems to have made grants to monastic houses. He founded Kirkham Priory in 1122 and in 1131 he granted lands to Abbot Bernard of Clairvaux, for the establishment of Rievaulx Abbey, the first northern Cistercian house in England, in 1132. There is some evidence to suggest that he was a highly literate man and, as might be expected for a man of his standing, he was a patron of scholarly study. Although no illustrations of Espec survive, he is remembered in a Yorkshire ballad as a man of considerable stature, being as 'large as the mountaine oake'. Espec's contemporary, Aelred, Abbot of Rievaulx, described his appearance in later life, noting 'black hair, a long beard, a broad open brow, large piercing eyes' and a 'gigantic' stature. He was also praised for his 'sonorous voice' and a 'wise and loyal' character.

A medieval arrowhead, found in the castle, which could have been used for hunting or warfare

while the rock, from those parts that were quarried, was used in the construction of many of the castle buildings. The subsequent lords of Helmsley might have adapted the ditches and ramparts to provide a formal approach around the castle (see pages 24–5). If the ditches were ever intended to hold water they have retained little evidence for this. However, one ditch, excavated to the north of the castle, was found to be lined with clay, a method usually used to prevent water from soaking away.

The outer ditch is defined by the smaller rampart to your left, which you have had to cross in order to enter the ditch. The larger rampart to the right masks a further inner ditch. As you follow the line of the ditch, you approach the castle through a former southern enclosure or bailey (indicated by the raised area), as the medieval visitor would have done. To the east is the 18th-century road to Duncombe Park, called Buckingham Square (named after the Dukes of Buckingham, who lived at Helmsley in the 17th century). Early maps suggest that in order to create this route it was necessary to cut through the southern portion of the medieval bailey, reducing it in size.

The modern path leads you to the south barbican and gate.

THE SOUTH BARBICAN

The south barbican provided an impressive, military façade for important visitors to the castle. It was built in the early 13th century by either Robert de Roos II (lord of Helmsley 1190–1227) or William de Roos I (lord of Helmsley 1227–58), and consisted of a stone curtain wall, four D-shaped towers and a gate. It was subsequently remodelled by William de Roos III (lord of Helmsley 1316–42) in the early 14th century.

The towers of the barbican originally had arrow slits, some of which were subsequently blocked or enlarged to form windows. The upper parts of the walls include a row of rectangular holes, which would have held timber beams. These beams supported a projecting wooden fighting gallery, or *hourd*, which ran along the whole length of the barbican, providing defenders with a way of

controlling the ground in front of the barbican and at the base of the walls (see page 29). While these features enhanced the architectural impact of the building, they also demonstrated the lord's knowledge of the latest military fashion to any visitor.

In the 13th century, the gatehouse consisted of two D-shaped towers, with a gateway set back between them. The *hourd* would have spanned the space between the towers, protecting the gate and providing a means of operating the drawbridge, which spanned the outer ditch. However, in the 14th century, the gate was altered by filling in the space between the two towers, creating a

Opposite: The inner ditch and castle ramparts from the south. This section of the ditch has been cut through the rock on which the castle stands

Below: The south barbican gatehouse. The right-hand 13th-century tower has had one of its arrow slits completely blocked by the addition of a latrine chute in the 14th century

JOHN GOODALL

The decorated interior of the south barbican gate passage

longer gate passage, with a new drawbridge mechanism and a latrine and stone chute where the north-east tower meets the curtain wall. The yellow sandstone used for this work contrasts with the surrounding 13th-century masonry.

As you enter the gate passage and look above your head, you will see two rectangular holes, and, in the flanking walls, a pair of slots. These formed part of the mechanism for raising and lowering the drawbridge

by a system of pulleys and ropes, operated from the room above. This drawbridge arrangement, the vaulting and the decorated stonework within the gate passage all date from the 14th century. However, at the end of the passage, the original 13th-century gate arch remains. Notice how the gate passage is aligned towards the south gate and the east tower beyond, signalling the route for the medieval visitor to take.

After passing through the gate passage, turn left and follow the inner face of the barbican wall.

Like many castle towers built in this period, the barbican towers were originally open-backed and had no residential function. But in the 14th century, William de Roos III added buildings against the inner face of the barbican wall, and chambers were created within the towers, probably to form lodgings for the steward or constable of the castle.

The wall footings of the 14th-century buildings can still be seen against the barbican wall. The principal room, between the gatehouse and south-west tower, had a fireplace and a latrine, both inserted into the fabric of the 13th-century curtain wall. The rear of the south-west tower was enclosed to form a small room, while the south-west gatehouse tower had its two arrow loops modified, one to form a fireplace and the other a drain.

ROBERT DE ROOS ❖ (FURSAN) ❖

The first major rebuilding at Helmsley was carried out by Robert de Roos II, also known as Fursan. Robert enjoyed a powerful political career, reflected in his marriage to Isabel, the illegitimate daughter of King Malcolm of Scots. He was also included among the twenty-five barons chosen to ensure that King John observed Magna Carta. Robert went on crusade to the Holy Land and was present when the Yorkshire contingent unsuccessfully assaulted Acre in 1190. He later became a member of the Knights Templar, a religious order, which was founded to protect pilgrims in the Holy Land. The Chartulary of Rievaulx records that Robert, 'raised the castles of Helmislay and of Wark', and it is likely that he undertook these works in order to create a suitably grand residence. Robert died in 1227 and was buried in the Temple Church in London.

Robert de Roos II's tomb effigy in the Temple Church, London

Retrace your steps and turn left to cross the modern bridge towards the south gate.

THE SOUTH GATE

The south gate formed one of the entrances to the inner bailey of Robert de Roos II's castle in the late 12th century. Although ruinous, its original appearance can be visualised by comparison with the slightly earlier gatehouse at Newark Castle. Like Newark, the gatehouse would have consisted of a rectangular tower pierced by a wide passageway. When the south barbican was added in the early 13th century, the south gate was also remodelled to include steps down into the inner ditch and further steps, to the south-west, which led up to a new gallery across the front of the gate.

The modern bridge in front of the gate replaces a drawbridge, which would have spanned the inner ditch. As you cross the bridge, you can see the two 14th-century wing-walls, which linked the south barbican with the inner bailey curtain wall and south gate. A further D-shaped tower was constructed at the end of the east wing-wall.

Within the gate passage there is a slot on the left-hand side, which would have held a portcullis, with a corresponding slot on the right. Beyond the portcullis was a double-leaf door, as indicated by the pivots

on either side. As you leave the gate passage, the small chamber on the right served as a porter's lodge or guardroom. Adjacent to this is the masonry base of a staircase, which provided access to the upper floors of the gatehouse and the curtain wall parapet-walk.

THE INNER BAILEY

Passing from the south gate, the visitor enters the inner bailey. In Espec's time, the bailey was divided into two separate enclosures by a large masonry wall, probably with a ditch, which ran between the positions of the east and west towers. Subsequently, the wall was largely demolished and the ditch filled, when Robert de Roos II added the east and

JONATHAN CLARK

Above: The north gatehouse at Newark Castle. Although Helmsley's south gate is slightly later in date, it would have looked similar to this

Below: The remains of the south gate and drawbridge. Beneath the drawbridge (replaced by the modern bridge) doorways led into the ditch and onto the ramparts

west towers. This created one large bailey, but some subdivision was retained by dividing it into three smaller courts, reflecting different uses of areas within the castle. You are standing in the first court that most medieval visitors would have encountered, and one of the more public areas of the castle.

BRITISH LIBRARY Add.ms.42130.f206v

A 14th-century illustration from the Luttrell Psalter *of meat being turned on a spit*

The Kitchen

The kitchen and other domestic service buildings were not just utilitarian; they were an important indicator of the lord's wealth and hospitality. These are located to your left, against the southern curtain wall. The first of these buildings is a kitchen, containing a large fireplace for cooking in its north-west wall, and ovens built into the fabric of the south gate. If you leave the kitchen following the curtain wall, you pass through an L-shaped passage, which leads into the great hall. On either side of the passage were the buttery and pantry, where food and drink would have been stored, before being

served in the hall. The stairs in the buttery area (to your left) lead to the basement of a tower, which was used for the storage of drink. These buildings date from the 14th century, and were built by either William de Roos II (lord of Helmsley 1285–1316) or William de Roos III, but they probably replace similar buildings in this area.

Passing between the buttery and pantry, continue along into the hall.

The Hall

You are now entering the former 'screens passage' of the hall. Medieval halls were governed by an internal hierarchy, with the public entrance and service areas located at the 'low' end and the lord's table and the private entrance at the 'high' end. You are currently standing in the 'low' end. As a guest, you would have entered the hall through the doorway to your right, rather than passing through the service area. Originally, a timber screen would have divided this entrance area from the main body of the hall (hence the term 'screens passage').

The hall was built against the 12th-century curtain wall, replacing an earlier hall. The later hall was probably aisled, and the original bay spacing is indicated by a series of ashlar piers built against the curtain wall. These provided additional strength to support timber wall posts which, in turn, would have helped to support the steeply pitched roof structure. A drain to take the rain-water and part of the seating for the roof can be traced, inserted into the curtain wall and west tower.

The north-west end wall includes a narrow offset on its internal face, which would have supported a raised timber platform, known as a dais, on which the lord and his family would have been seated. In front of the dais was an open central hearth, vented through a louvre in the roof. The doorway in the west corner provided private access for the lord, his family and privileged guests to apartments contained in the west tower and chamber block. It is no longer possible to pass this way, as the vault which spanned the stairs to the basement of the west tower has been lost.

A 13th-century French manuscript illustration of a lord being served at high table

BRITISH LIBRARY Add.ms.28162.f10v

A reconstruction drawing, by Philip Corke, of the interior of the hall in the 14th century, looking towards the high end, and the lord's table

Right: The basement of the west tower. As the vault was constructed, the ribs and rubble stonework would have been supported by 'centering', consisting of a timber frame and woven willow. The centering held the stones in place until the mortar set and was then removed, but the impressions left by the willow weave can still be seen

Below: The west tower, seen from the site of the hall. The stub of masonry projecting from the corner of the tower is part of the curtain wall, and indicates the wall's original height

Leave the hall and walk towards the west tower.

THE WEST TOWER

The lower portion of the west tower was constructed between 1190 and 1200 by Robert de Roos II, as a three-storey block, containing residential rooms on its ground and first floors and a basement for storage. The basement of the west tower was built within a ditch, and its north-west wall was constructed on top of a large wall running across the bailey towards the east tower. The wall and ditch had been built during Walter Espec's time and once divided the inner bailey into two separate enclosures. The tower was heightened in the 14th century by William de Roos II or III, and the south-west wall was rebuilt, projecting into the inner ditch. Rooms were now provided on three floors. The tower was further remodelled in the 16th century, when an additional floor was inserted by lowering the 14th-century floor levels. However, the function of the tower remained the same, providing a series of private rooms for the lord and his family.

Go down the stairs into the basement of the west tower.

This basement was probably used for storage, and it is unlikely to have been heated. A narrow window with seats provided a little light, and with rendered and lime-washed walls, this would have been a brighter and more pleasant place than it appears today. If you look carefully at the ends of the arch above the window seats, you can see a pair of peacocks' heads, an

emblem of the Roos family. The final bay of the vault to the south-west was added in the 14th century, when the tower was extended.

Retrace your steps to ground level.

The ground floor of the tower is reached via a short flight of steps, through a round-headed, 12th-century doorway. Directly above the door is a large, 16th-century window and above this, the blocked remains of a 12th-century lancet window.

Go through the doorway into the tower.

The south-west wall at ground-floor level includes a 14th-century door to a latrine and a window with seats. The upper floors were remodelled in the 16th century, with large mullioned and transomed windows flanking central fireplaces. Further 14th-century windows on the first and second floors were blocked when the later fireplaces were inserted. The opposite wall has been treated in a similar fashion. However, at ground-floor level is an original, late 12th-century fireplace incorporating a later 'keeping-hole' (a place to keep items dry). The blocked remains of a further fireplace can be seen at first-floor level.

The south-east wall has a further 14th-century window, again with seats, at ground-floor level. A stone corbel and rows of sockets once supported the timber beams for the 16th-century floors, each room being lit by a

mullioned and transomed window. In the western corner is a series of tall, 14th-century doorways, leading into latrines. Their floor levels were lowered in the 16th century, so that they could be reached from the new floors. On the opposite wall can be seen a series of doors, which lead to a spiral staircase; this runs the full height of the tower, from the first floor upwards. This is part of the 14th-century arrangement by William de Roos II or III, but in order for the stairs to match the new 16th-century levels, a strip of masonry was added to the north elevation, with door openings constructed at the appropriate levels. From ground level, the stairs were reached through the 14th-century doorway in the centre of the wall, and a further straight flight of stairs.

Leave the west tower and approach the east tower. On your right is the castle well covered with a vault, while on your left (west) are the remains of the chapel.

The interior south corner of the west tower. The ground-floor 14th-century window has been altered to accommodate the 16th-century fireplace above

The east tower from the castle bailey. The 14th-century heightening of the tower can be seen in the use of different coloured stone. Rows of small rectangular holes were used to secure the scaffolding as the tower was being built. Although these are now visible, they would have been blocked and covered by rendering once work had been completed

THE EAST TOWER

Although ruinous, the east tower is the most prominent feature of the castle today. It was built by Robert de Roos II, and its location, scale and orientation suggest that it was intended to be seen from the town as a potent symbol of the lord's wealth and power. The rooms in the east tower were also designed to impress; the main room possibly acted as the lord's receiving

chamber, in which he conducted estate business. In the 18th century, the east tower was appropriated as a Romantic ruin, set in the grounds of Duncombe Park.

The west end of the building is rectangular, but the east wall is circular on the outside and faceted on the inside. In the late 12th century, the tower consisted of a vaulted basement with a large room above. Originally, the upper room was reached by external doorways, accessed via stairs against the curtain wall. Both doorways have external hood-mouldings, but the one in the south-east wall appears to have been the public entrance, as it faces the south gate. In addition, both of these doors would have provided access onto the parapet walk on the curtain wall.

During the 14th century, however, the tower was heightened and four floors were created. This heightening can be seen on the outside of the tower, and is marked by the use of yellow sandstone.

Enter the basement through the south-east door.

The basement is now entered via a 14th-century doorway cut through the south-east wall; originally, the vaulted basement was reached by means of a circular staircase from the upper floor in the western corner of the building. At basement level, the south-west wall has two window loops in splayed embrasures and a

doorway to the stairs. In the 12th century, the upper floor would have been lit by three tall lancet windows, which are still visible today. Above is a smaller lancet and the line of the steeply pitched, original roof. The parapet would have risen above the height of the roof. The opposite wall was largely destroyed in the 17th century, but the rounded base, containing a further embrasure and postern gate, can still be traced.

When the tower was heightened in the 14th century, a further vault was inserted, dividing the 12th-century upper room into two levels. The vault springing can be seen above the three large lancet windows in the south-west wall and in the two remaining corners. Above the vault, the new room had a timber ceiling, running at the same level as the apex of the 12th-century roof. The original stairs were extended by an extra flight to reach the new room. The splay of the north-west lancet window was cut back and its sill was raised, in order to accommodate this extension. From the new room, a spiral staircase in the north-west wall, reached by a short timber staircase, provided access to a further room above and to the parapet walk. The upper room was an attic chamber, with a hipped roof and a timber floor (the ceiling of the room below), and a blind arcade on the south-west wall.

The parapet walk was paved and had crenellated parapets, visible today.

The turrets, or bartizans, which were added to the tower's two corners, are slightly different. The turret on the north-west had a lead roof, while the one on the south-east had a flagged upper floor. The interiors of both turrets were reached through doors off the parapet walk.

Following a serious fire in the late 14th century, the timber floor of the upper chamber was replaced with a stone vault, and the roof was rebuilt. With each of these developments, some re-planning of the stairs and wall passages was necessary. In addition, with each remodelling, some of the original 12th-century windows were either blocked or modified to suit the new floor and ceiling levels.

Leave the east tower and enter the chapel.

THE CHAPEL

The chapel effectively forms the north-east enclosure wall of Robert de Roos II's central court. The position of this building was dictated by the presence of the east tower at the north-east corner of the central court and by the early dividing ditch and wall of the inner bailey, upon which the east wall of the chapel appears to have been built. As would be expected, the chapel is orientated east to west along its main axis. A new castle chapel was consecrated in 1246, suggesting that the current building had been established by this date.

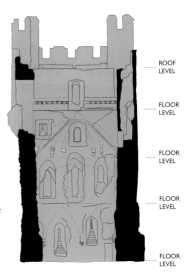

ROOF LEVEL

FLOOR LEVEL

FLOOR LEVEL

FLOOR LEVEL

FLOOR LEVEL

■ 1190–1227
■ 1285–1342
□ Late 14th century

A section of the east tower showing the position of the vaults and the main phases of development

Above: These floor tiles from Rievaulx Abbey are similar to the ones that would have been used in the chapel at Helmsley

Below: The chamber block and latrine tower viewed along the remains of the first-floor gallery. Most of the windows date from Edward Manners's remodelling of the castle buildings

The surviving remains of the chapel indicate that it was a highly decorated building. There were two doorways at either end of the south wall and a further doorway at the east end of the north wall. The bases of angle buttresses survive on two corners. When the chapel was excavated, floor tiles, similar to those found at Rievaulx Abbey, were uncovered, in addition to painted window glass. The chapel has a recess at its eastern end; this would have accommodated a reredos (a screen or panelling) behind the altar. Part of the moulded jamb of a tall window survives in the south-east corner. The western end of the chapel was adapted in the 16th century, to incorporate a balcony accessible from a gallery running

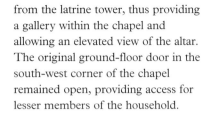

from the latrine tower, thus providing a gallery within the chapel and allowing an elevated view of the altar. The original ground-floor door in the south-west corner of the chapel remained open, providing access for lesser members of the household.

Leave the chapel and approach the chamber block on the other side of the courtyard.

THE CHAMBER BLOCK

Although traditionally interpreted as a hall, this building is more likely to have formed a 12th-century chamber block, associated with a detached hall and service range, located on the site of the 14th-century hall and services. A similar arrangement, if slightly later in date, can be seen at Scarborough Castle (also in the care of English Heritage). At first-floor level, the chamber block would have consisted of two rooms: a great chamber at the south-east end, and a more private, inner chamber to the north-west, which had direct access to a set of garderobes. The ground floor, or undercroft, would probably have been used for storage.

The building's current appearance is due mainly to the remodelling by Edward Manners, between 1563 and 1587. While the west tower provided the private apartments, the former chamber block was redesigned as a series of state apartments. The ground floor contained an entrance hall at its south-east end, with service rooms to the north-west, while the first floor had a great chamber or dining room and a more private room. The chamber block was further remodelled and the rooms subdivided in the late 17th century, but many of these alterations were reversed in the early 20th century.

Look up at the outside of the chamber block as you make your way towards the wooden stairs at the south-east end.

The four mullioned and transomed windows at first-floor level, and the smaller windows at ground-floor level, date from Edward Manners's remodelling of the building, but some 12th-century features survive. At the north-west end, directly above the small door into the ground floor, is the jamb of a door opening. Towards the centre of the building, at ground-floor level, is the base of a window. Next to the wooden stairs is a masonry projection, which would have supported a flue and a fireplace at first-floor level. Finally, beneath the wooden stairs, there is a blocked, round-headed doorway, with moulded decoration, which led to the undercroft.

Enter the chamber block through the doorway beneath the wooden stairs.

During Edward Manners's time, the ground floor was divided into three rooms by timber and plaster partitions. This first room was the largest, and formed the entrance hall in the Tudor period. A survey of 1636 suggests that this room contained two long tables, a cupboard and four 'forms' (long benches, which would run along either side of the tables). The room still has a large fireplace and a window in the north-east wall, and two more windows in the opposite wall. The door opening in the south-east wall has been forced through to

The Tudor entrance hall to the chamber block

❖ EDWARD MANNERS ❖

Edward Manners, the third Earl of Rutland and fifteenth Lord Roos of Helmsley, succeeded to the lordship of Helmsley in 1563, following the death of his father, Henry. Edward was socially ambitious and he made an advantageous marriage to Isabel Holcroft, daughter of Sir Thomas Holcroft of Vale Royal, Cheshire. Edward held many political offices during his lifetime, gaining considerable wealth and prestige. He was appointed Lord Chancellor in 1587, but had held the position for only two days when he suddenly died. His daughter Elizabeth was his only heir and was later to pass the Barony of Roos to her husband, William Cecil, Lord Burghley.

The arms of Edward Manners, third Earl of Rutland, which decorate the first floor of the chamber block

A medieval green glass bottle, used for storing oils and perfumes

Below: One of the Tudor service rooms on the ground floor of the chamber block

Below right: A stool pot from the 16th or 17th century, discovered in the castle. It would have been used at night and emptied in the morning

the 14th-century stairs of the west tower. The offset in the north-east wall, which supported the timbers of the 12th-century first floor, can be seen beneath the current ceiling.

Leave the room through the door in the timber partition.

The central room contains an original, 12th-century circular staircase in its south-west wall; the doorway dates from the 16th century. These stairs go down to a doorway, which once led to a timber bridge spanning the inner ditch. The stairs would also have continued up to first-floor level, but the upper flight was blocked and removed during the 16th-century remodelling. The opposite wall has a 16th-century fireplace and window.

Leave the room through the door in the next timber partition.

The third ground-floor room would have been a service room, with windows in the outer walls, and a door in the north-east wall leading into a further service building.

Leave the ground floor through the door in the north-west corner and go up the stone stairs into the latrine tower.

THE LATRINE TOWER

The latrine tower was remodelled several times and, as such, is a highly complex part of the castle. It was originally built by Robert de Roos II, when Walter Espec's early 12th-century chamber block was being remodelled. Initially, it consisted of a small building containing the private latrines that served the chamber block. In the 14th century, the interior was remodelled, to provide the elaborate pair of latrines that can be seen today. In the 16th century, both the north-east and north-west walls were largely dismantled and rebuilt, creating a much larger tower with rooms on three floors. Some further alterations,

❖ TUDOR LIFE AT HELMSLEY ❖

The arrangement and use of rooms and spaces at Helmsley in Tudor times differed little from the medieval period; the great chamber and hall were still important, ceremonial rooms. However, the medieval great hall was replaced with a smaller, single-storey hall on the ground floor of the chamber block, which would have served as the servants' dining room and entrance hall. But the hall remained the first state room that the visitor would have entered.

Like its medieval predecessor, the great chamber was located on the first floor of the chamber block and would have been used for dining, music and dancing, and as a setting for plays. It would have been as richly decorated and as large as the hall on the ground floor. Adjoining the great chamber would have been a withdrawing chamber, for private sitting and eating.

HADDON HALL

One innovation in larger houses was the introduction of long galleries, probably originating in design from earlier covered walkways. The remains of one still exist at Helmsley, between the chapel and the chamber block. The long gallery not only served as a covered route between different parts of the house, but also provided a space for indoor exercise, and for activities such as masques, games and music. It also allowed views across the castle courtyards and gardens to the north-west. The walls would have been decorated with paintings, portraits and tapestries, displaying not only ancestors, relations and friends, but also great people from the past and of the day. The walls would have been timber-panelled and the ceiling decorated, while fireplaces would have kept the occupants warm.

NATIONAL PORTRAIT GALLERY, LONDON

Above: The long gallery at Haddon Hall. Built by Sir George Vernon in the mid-16th century, the gallery's present appearance can be attributed to the remodelling by Sir John Manners

Left: A detail of a feast scene from a portrait of Sir Henry Unton, c.1596, showing Tudor hospitality on a grand scale

The 14th-century latrines in the latrine tower. Their shafts discharged into the castle's inner ditch

vaulted passage from the chamber block. Above the vault was a staircase, which rose against the south-east wall. To the right is the base of the original wall of the latrine building. During rebuilding in the 16th century, fireplaces and windows were provided within the new walls. However, further alterations became necessary in order to provide access to the first-floor gallery to the chapel.

Leave the latrine tower through the door on the left. You are now on the first floor of the chamber block.

The first floor is divided into two rooms, both retaining some of their 16th-century fittings. This first room has fragments of a decorative plaster frieze and a 16th-century stone fireplace. The round-headed, late 12th-century doorway originally led

particularly to the upper floor, took place in the 17th century.

The 14th-century latrines remain in the south-west wall, lit by a pair of loop windows built into the masonry. These would have been divided by a timber partition, which has since been removed. Each latrine was provided with its own locker. To the left of the latrines are the remains of a

Fragments of the sumptuous Tudor interior survive in this first-floor room of the chamber block

The painted frieze is decorated with the arms of the third Earl of Rutland, and with mermaids, dolphins and fleur-de-lis

to the latrine tower. This doorway was blocked during the 16th-century remodelling and a new door was cut into the north corner of the room.

Go through into the next room.

This room has a plaster ceiling of polygonal panels, containing knots and roses, and a painted frieze decorated with mermaids and the third earl's arms. Some of the decorated timber panelling remains, as well as a fine fireplace, dated 1582.

Leave the first floor of the chamber block through the door in the east corner of the room and go down the wooden stairs.

The 16th-century remodelling of the chamber block included the construction of a timber loggia along its north-east side. The loggia's timber posts were supported on a series of stone bases, which can be seen running parallel to the chamber block wall, along with the stone base

of a staircase which led up to a first-floor gallery. The whole structure would have been quite open, to allow light to flood into the chamber block.

Walk over to the remains of the first-floor gallery.

Linked to the loggia was the first-floor gallery to the chapel, which was partly constructed on earlier walls. The upper portion of the south-east wall would have been mainly of timber, but it would have incorporated large windows to provide views across the inner court. The north-west wall has two rectangular masonry bases, which supported the chimneys and fireplaces that heated the gallery. Adjacent to these are the bases of latrine chutes, provided with apertures for cleaning. These served small latrines or closets constructed off the main gallery.

As you leave the inner court through the middle of the former gallery, you enter the northern court of the inner bailey.

Far right: A miller and his wife carrying flour from their mill, from the Luttrell Psalter. *The lords of Helmsley had their own water-powered mill on the River Rye*

THE SECOND SERVICE AREA: BREWHOUSE AND BAKEHOUSE

This part of the castle would have provided an additional service area. Along the south-west side are the remains of a bakehouse and brewhouse, with the bases for ovens. A building runs at a right-angle to these; it might once have been a storehouse or granary. The wall-footings of a further building can be seen against the northern stretch of curtain wall. Although little evidence remains for its form, its location suggests that it might have served as a stable.

Between the stable, east tower and chapel are the remains of a range of 16th-century buildings. Like the first-floor gallery, they would have been mainly timber-framed. It is difficult to be certain of their function, but at least one of the ground-floor rooms included a fireplace, suggesting they might have served as additional accommodation.

Above: A 15th- or 16th-century bung hole pot or cistern. A tap in the bottom would have allowed drinks, such as ale, to be served

THE NORTHERN CURTAIN WALLS, TOWERS AND GATE

All of the these structures date from Robert de Roos II's time and represent a complete replacement of Walter Espec's work. Although ruined to a low level, they would have formed an impressive symmetrical façade to the northern face of the castle. The curtain walls were faced in rubble but, in contrast, all of the towers were faced with finely squared stones. The east tower was also

Right: Two of the ovens contained in the bakehouse

treated in the same way. Although all the towers have curved external faces, their interiors are generally faceted. The design of this façade is similar to some of the royal works of King John, particularly those in Ireland, such as Dublin and Limerick Castles, which all date from the first two decades of the 13th century.

A series of loops in the curtain wall overlooked the inner ditch, but most of these were subsequently blocked. In the north corner, the curtain wall terminates in an unusual circular tower, which includes a smaller circular turret on its north front. (This is best seen from the rampart.) The turret would probably have been taller than the rest of the tower, in order to provide a more elevated viewing point, and perhaps a position from which to fly the lord's banner. There is a postern gate along this stretch of curtain wall, between the tower and the north gate.

Leave the inner bailey of the castle via the north gate.

The north gate consisted of two D-shaped towers, flanking a gate passage. The rebate for a door and portcullis to close off the gate passage is still visible. The modern timber bridge replaces a drawbridge, which would have spanned the inner ditch. Stairs within the drawbridge pit lead to a doorway into the inner ditch. (A similar arrangement is found in the south gate.)

THE NORTH BARBICAN

Like the south gate, the north gate was enhanced with a barbican, added either by William de Roos I or Robert de Roos III (lord of Helmsley 1258–85). This consisted of a pair of drum towers flanking a central passage, their outer walls extending back to form a small enclosure. Like the south barbican, the rear of the north barbican would have been open and had no residential function. The abutment for a drawbridge can still be seen on the counter-lip of the outer ditch.

The remains of the north barbican

THE EXTERIOR OF THE WEST RANGE

If you have time, cross the north barbican wall to your left as you leave the castle, and follow the rampart round, where a greater appreciation can be gained of the castle's defences and main domestic buildings.

On the left are the remains of the western corner tower; a chamfered plinth runs around its base. To the south of this, a substantial portion of the curtain wall survives. Beyond the curtain wall are the latrine tower and chamber block. The 16th-century alterations to the west wall of the chamber block include mullioned and transomed windows, and the projecting windows, which provided excellent views of the surrounding medieval deer parks. The round-headed doorway near the bottom of the block would have led to a timber bridge across the inner ditch, to the rampart on which you are standing. Clearly visible in the wall of the west tower are the central, 14th-century windows and loop. The upper two have been blocked, while the lower two remain open and still incorporate their original ironwork.

You can either return to the north gate and barbican and explore the medieval route around the castle or follow the bank round and leave by the south barbican.

HISTORY OF THE CASTLE

HELMSLEY BEFORE THE CASTLE

At the time of the Norman Conquest, Helmsley was only a small town, surrounded by forests and arable lands. It is recorded in Domesday Book as 'Elmeslac' and was variously known in later centuries as 'Haumesley', 'Haumelac', 'Hamelak' and 'Helmeslegh'. Following William the Conqueror's attacks on the North, the lands surrounding Helmsley were laid waste, leaving only the settlements of Helmsley and Byland with priests. The manor of Helmsley was subsequently granted to the king's half-brother, Robert de Mortain, but was confiscated by the Crown in 1088, following De Mortain's plot to overthrow the king. Although not recorded, it is possible that De Mortain had established a castle on the current site. The castle would have been either in the form of a 'ring-work', a simple ditch and rampart enclosure, or a 'motte and bailey', an earth mound surmounted by a timber tower within a ditch and rampart enclosure.

The castle, seen from Duncombe Park

LANDSCAPES OF LOR
❖ The castle and

Medieval lords demonstrated their wealth and power in a variety of ways. They wore fine clothes and had rare or expensive possessions; they built impressive castles; they administered justice; they gave and received hospitality; and they participated in distinctive activities, pre-eminently hunting. Many of these activities can be traced in the archaeology and architecture of a particular site. New research has indicated that Helmsley Castle was set within a landscape carefully contrived to enhance the power and status of the lord, in all his various pursuits.

A hunting scene from a medieval manuscript by Gaston Phebus

The west, south and south-east sides of the castle were enclosed by a private parkland, used for hunting and recreation, which formed a complete contrast to the bustling town and public spaces to the east and north (see the map opposite). There were two separate parks. One was attached to the west side of the castle. Its inner enclosure was known as 'La Haye', and it formed almost an amphitheatre on the slope of the hill outside the windows of the private apartments of the castle, with woodlands forming an enclosing backdrop. This was subsequently extended, and became the West or New Park. Since the 18th century, it has formed part of the estate of Duncombe Park. The larger East or Old Park lay a short distance away to the south-east. A straight route linked it, via a ford across the River Rye, to the castle. The architectural sequence of the two southern gateways and the east tower continued this line into the castle.

The last section of this route – from where it crossed the road to York – also provided an impressive approach to the castle, perhaps intended for the lord and his most important visitors. They would have had views of the skyline of the castle, leading the way to the south gate.

The layout of the castle was not static, however. It became increasingly elaborate, especially in the later medieval period. Gardens and orchards were created to the north, blocking and diverting main roads that had once lain outside the main north gate. The final stages of the southern approach to the castle were also altered, probably in the 13th century (see the diagram opposite), to create a route around the earthworks, designed to impress visitors with the scale and opulence of the buildings and their setting, and to reinforce the power of the lord.

HIP AND PLEASURE:
ndscape setting ❖

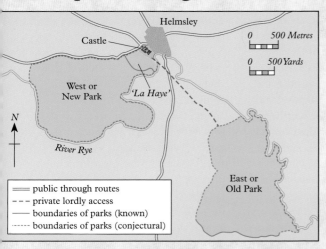

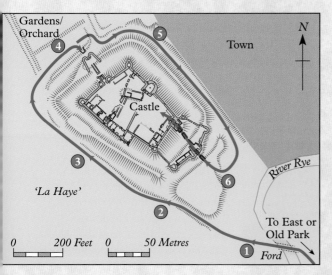

Left: Helmsley Castle and its medieval hunting parks

Below: A diagram showing the later medieval access to the castle

1 From the river ford, visitors were led not directly to the south gate, but along the west side of the south forecourt, via an easier, ramped route.

2 Glimpse through the inner bank, which has now been filled in, of the south-west tower on the curtain wall and the exposed, rocky outcrop. Oblique view along the façade of the south barbican.

3 Views of the castle's most impressive residential accommodation. The inner park, 'La Haye', lay to the left.

4 Choice between entering the north gate (former principal public entrance) or continuing east and south by dropping down into the outer ditch.

5 The north-east corner tower and east tower would have loomed impressively over the route southwards, leading the visitor on.

6 The axial entry through the southern gatehouses would have made a dramatic impression on the visitor, with the east tower straight ahead and the great hall across the court to the west.

By Paul Everson and P. S. Barnwell

WALTER ESPEC AND THE CASTLE

The history of Helmsley in the early years of the 12th century only becomes clear with the grant of the manor and other lands formerly held by De Mortain to Walter Espec in 1120. Espec was one of the most prominent nobles in England at this time, holding many royal positions, including Justiciar of the Northern Counties, and commanding an army in support of King Stephen at the Battle of the Standard in 1138.

Espec either established or rebuilt the castle at Helmsley, on a rocky outcrop overlooking the River Rye. The castle was to serve as a residence

The interior of the east tower. Large sections of the tower remain in the inner ditch, after it was blown up following the Civil War

for Espec within his Yorkshire estates, and it is likely to have been constructed soon after his acquisition of the manor of Helmsley. The castle acted as Espec's principal residence until his death in 1154. The choice of this site probably arose from its location at the heart of Espec's Yorkshire estates, just as his castle at Wark was situated at the centre of his Northumbrian estates. Espec's castle at Helmsley was planned around two rectangular baileys, divided by a ditch and wall, and entered via a gateway from the north. Both baileys were protected by an external double ditch. A further, lesser gate would have been located to the south, while the main domestic buildings were located along the south-west side of the bailey. Masonry, earth and timber were used in the construction of the castle. The substantial earthwork defences were retained in later rebuilding works, and still survive today. Unlike most other castles of the period, Helmsley might have had no central motte (mound) to function as the main stronghold; instead, the buildings of the castle were ranged around the perimeter of its baileys.

Espec's time in royal service had earned him considerable wealth and landed estates, and he granted many of these to religious institutions. Espec's generosity to these foundations may be because he had no direct heir. A late medieval legend records that Espec had once had a son, but after his fatal fall from a horse, his father decided to make Christ heir to part of his lands through charitable donations. He founded Kirkham Priory, North Yorkshire, in 1122, and in 1131 he granted lands in Ryedale to Abbot Bernard of Clairvaux; Rievaulx Abbey, the first northern Cistercian house, was founded on this property in the following year. (Both these abbeys are in the care of English Heritage.) A further grant of lands in Bedfordshire led to the creation of a daughter house at Warden Abbey in 1136.

Following his death in 1154, Espec's estates passed to his sister's husband, Peter de Roos and, by about 1157, his son Robert was in possession of Espec's lands. Helmsley Castle was to remain in the De Roos family until the 17th century.

FURSAN AND THE RAISING OF THE CASTLE

It was Robert's grandson, also called Robert, or Fursan (lord of Helmsley c.1186–1227), who rebuilt much of Helmsley Castle after 1186. The Chartulary of Rievaulx records that Fursan, 'raised the castles of Helmislay and of Wark', and many of his buildings are preserved at the core of the surviving castle, reflecting the wealth and power that he enjoyed. Married to the illegitimate daughter of King William of Scotland, he founded and endowed several religious houses and was one of the twenty-five

barons chosen to enforce Magna Carta in 1215. He also joined the Knights Templar, a religious order founded to protect pilgrims in the Holy Land, and was buried in the Temple Church in London, following his death in 1227.

Fursan's rebuilding involved a substantial enhancement and expansion of the castle's defences and domestic arrangements. In order to create space for the planned expansion, Fursan exchanged land with the monks of Rievaulx for holdings next to the town and south of the castle to the River Rye. Fursan's work initially focused on the southern part of the site, with the construction of a new south gate, which became the main entrance, sections of curtain wall and a round corner tower. Substantial domestic towers were erected to the east and west, within the ditch that had divided Espec's castle into two baileys. Furthermore, the wall that had divided the two baileys was largely dismantled, in order to turn Espec's two baileys into one. With the southern part of the site completed, the former northern bailey received attention, and Espec's chamber block was remodelled and a new north gate, curtain wall and corner towers were built in the latest style. Judging from the variations discernible in the masonry of some of Fursan's work, the building campaign must have been a prolonged one, perhaps not even completed by his death in 1227.

The gatehouse at Kirkham Priory, founded by Walter Espec

THE 13TH CENTURY

A reconstruction drawing, by Peter Dunn, of the castle in about 1300. The east tower has yet to be heightened, but it still dominates the castle

Fursan was succeeded by his son William de Roos I, who lived in the castle until his death in 1258. He finished the additions to the castle defences that his father had started, and erected a new chapel, consecrated in 1246. By William's time, the parks had been well established, with one to the south-east of the castle called the 'Old Park' and a further park to the west called 'La Haye'. The parks provided places of distraction and leisure, where the lord could entertain guests and pursue

recreational hunting, while also providing a source of luxury food such as deer. Both parks are mentioned in 1302 along with the 'Rapark', which was probably an orchard or garden to the north of the castle. Although the full extent of these parks is currently uncertain, the one called 'La Haye' covered, at least in part, the area occupied by the 18th-century Duncombe Park.

The standing of the De Roos was further improved by the marriage of William's son and successor, Robert, to Isabel Daubeney. By this marriage, he acquired Belvoir Castle in Leicestershire and was later made first Lord Roos of Hamlake. In keeping with his new-found status, Robert de Roos III undertook further improvements at Helmsley, adding a barbican to the north gate and remodelling Espec's south gate. Following Robert's death in 1285, his body was buried at Kirkham Priory and his heart at Croxden Abbey, Staffordshire (also in the care of English Heritage).

THE 14TH CENTURY

Robert's son, William de Roos II, succeeded to the titles of Lord Roos of Helmsley and Belvoir. He also enjoyed a socially advantageous marriage to Matilda de Vaux, heiress to half of the Vaux estates. William died in 1316 and Helmsley passed to his son, William de Roos III. Both Williams undertook a remodelling of the castle, improving its defences and domestic accommodation.

The southern barbican gate was strengthened by extending the gate passage, and accommodation was provided against the barbican wall, probably for the constable of the castle. At this time, the constable received 3d. a day and a robe to the value of 20s., as befitted his office. An extra storey with decorative angle turrets was added to the east tower.

This small Purbeck marble effigy was originally from Croxden Abbey, but it was moved at the Dissolution to St Mary's Church, Bottesford. It is possible that it represents Robert de Roos III, and that it was placed in the abbey church where his heart had been buried. Robert had acquired Belvoir Castle, Leicestershire, on his marriage, and the Roos family continued to assert its interests in the area by burying his heart at the nearby abbey at Croxden

A reconstruction drawing, by Philip Corke, of the south barbican in about 1300, showing the impressive approach that it provided to the castle

A reconstruction drawing, by Peter Dunn, of the castle in about 1585. The chamber block has been remodelled to form the core of the Tudor house. The medieval hall had probably been removed by this time

But their most radical works at Helmsley were the improvements to their own accommodation. A new hall was built, including a new kitchen and service range; the west tower was heightened and converted into apartments for the lord and his family; and a new brewhouse and

bakehouse were built in the north-east corner of the bailey. Some of these alterations might have been in preparation for King Edward III's visit to the castle in 1334, which would have required suitable lodgings for his retinue. It was estimated, at the end of William de Roos III's time,

that the castle could not be kept in good repair for less than 100s. a year, a large sum, reflecting the extent of the new accommodation.

These alterations at Helmsley reflect the late medieval development of the baronial household within a lord's castle. By the fourteenth century, such households were expanding in size, including greater numbers of retainers, all of whom had to be accommodated in chambers of appropriate status. The increase in accommodation at Helmsley provided for members of this expanded household, while retaining the privacy of the lord and his family. Such alterations often resulted in less emphasis on the defences of a castle, but it is unlikely that lords such as the De Roos would have regarded this as a compromise between defence and comfort. The lord of Helmsley would have impressed visitors in a number of ways. It was important, in a society in which warfare was a noble activity, that he display his knowledge of the latest military architecture, while demonstrating his power, wealth and status through domestic buildings, and lavish hospitality.

THE LATE MEDIEVAL LORDS AND TUDORS

Helmsley Castle remained with the De Roos family throughout the 14th and 15th centuries, until Thomas de Roos III took the Lancastrian side in the War of the Roses and, in 1461, he was attainted (certain rights were removed for this act of high treason). In the following years, the castle became a dower house, but after Thomas was beheaded following the Battle of Hexham in 1464, it passed to the Crown. The castle was then granted to George, Duke of Clarence, and after his death in 1478, to his brother Richard, Duke of Gloucester (later Richard III). Richard is not thought to have lived at Helmsley and, following his death at the Battle of Bosworth in 1485, the castle and its associated estates were restored to Edmund de Roos, the eleventh Lord Roos. Throughout his lifetime, Edmund's estates were governed

Part of a 15th-century illustration, showing George, Duke of Clarence, from the Rous Roll, *a genealogy of the Earls of Warwick*

BRITISH LIBRARY Add.ms48976

A reconstruction drawing, by Philip Corke, showing the hall and kitchen in about 1300

Above: A fanciful 19th-century engraving of the interior of the chamber block when it was inhabited by the Manners family

Below: Rievaulx Abbey, which was purchased by Thomas Manners after the Dissolution. Some stonework from Rievaulx was reused to create the Tudor house at Helmsley

by Sir Thomas Lovell, as Edmund, 'was not of sufficient disscrecion to guyde himself and his lyvelode'. Edmund was the last direct member of the De Roos family to hold Helmsley, and he died without heir in 1508, being succeeded by his nephew, Sir George Manners of Etal in Northumberland. George's son, Thomas Manners, succeeded to the title in 1513 and was a strong supporter of the Tudor dynasty, being rewarded with the earldom of Rutland in 1525. His support for the Crown did not falter during the religious upheaval of the 1530s, when Henry VIII broke with the Catholic Church, as demonstrated by his assistance in the removal of Abbot Edward of Rievaulx in 1533. His loyalty to the Crown was further recognised by his purchase, at very favourable rates, of the site and estates of Rievaulx and other former monastic estates in Yorkshire and Leicestershire.

Thomas was directly associated with Helmsley, although he made few alterations to the castle. It was not until the accession of his grandson, Edward Manners, third Earl of Rutland (Lord Roos 1563–87), that significant building works were carried out. It is probable that these works were prompted by Edward's marriage to Isabel Holcroft, as is suggested by the use of their heraldic symbols in the surviving decorative plasterwork in the chamber block. The 12th-century chamber block, west tower and latrine tower were adapted to create chambers and state apartments, while a first-floor gallery was created between the chamber block and the chapel. Some of the medieval buildings, such as the hall, were probably demolished at this time and the materials reused, while additional materials were obtained from Rievaulx Abbey. The work did not proceed smoothly; a workman obtaining stone from Rievaulx was discharged for his conduct in 1577. Manners was told in April 1578 that his 'buildings at the Castle here do not proceed so speedily as the mason supposed', and the mason's work would not be finished before August. However, by 1582, the works appear to have been completed and a new Tudor mansion created.

Francis Manners, sixth Earl of Rutland, died in 1632, when the estates passed through Katherine, Duchess of Buckingham and Lady Roos

(Katherine Manners) eventually to her eldest son George Villiers, who became second Duke of Buckingham in 1648. There is little evidence in this period that the castle was occupied until the outbreak of the Civil War.

THE CIVIL WAR AND AFTERMATH

During the Civil War, Helmsley was garrisoned by Royalist troops. The Parliamentarian siege of Helmsley, from September to November 1644, was the castle's first and last military engagement. Attempts to lift the siege by Royalist troops from Knaresborough were unsuccessful and, in November 1644, Sir Jordan Crosland, the governor of Helmsley Castle, was forced to surrender due to lack of food. It was, however, a surrender with honour and Crosland's men were allowed to march out with their small arms. Many of the Royalist soldiers went on join the Parliamentarian army. The Parliamentarian commander in charge of the siege, Sir Thomas Fairfax, was instructed to 'slight' Helmsley, and he partially dismantled the curtain walls and towers and blew

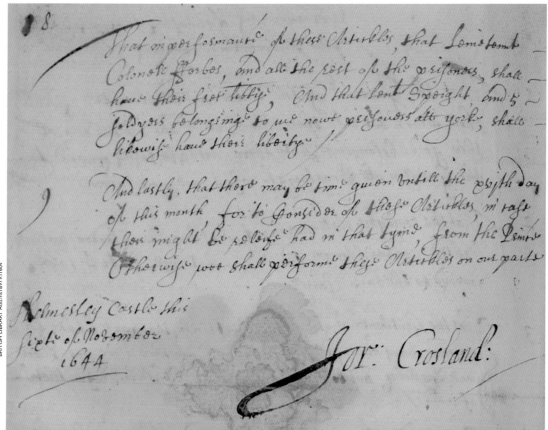

Above: A spur, dating from the Civil War, found at Helmsley

Below: A letter written by Sir Jordan Crosland at Helmsley to Lord Fairfax, listing his proposals for the surrender of the castle, dated 6 November 1644

❖ THOMAS FAIRFAX ❖

Thomas Fairfax was born in Wharfedale, Yorkshire, in 1612, and joined the army following an education at Cambridge. He progressed quickly through the ranks and was knighted in about 1639 for his role in the campaign against the Scottish Covenanters, who were resisting the political and church reforms imposed from London. Following the outbreak of the Civil War, Fairfax fought for the Parliamentarians, and he was appointed commander-in-chief of Cromwell's New Model Army in 1645. Fairfax led successful campaigns, such as the siege of York and the Battle of Naseby, building a

A 17th-century illustration of Thomas Fairfax, shown at the head of the table

BRITISH LIBRARY Shelf mark G 3861

reputation as an excellent military leader. Such victories in the field, however, did not turn Fairfax into a ruthless conqueror, and he secured the protection of the Bodleian Library in Oxford, as well as the churches and stained glass in York. His military pre-eminence won him lands and wealth, including Helmsley Castle, and he passed these to his only heir, his daughter Mary. Rather than lead Cromwell's army into Scotland in 1650, Fairfax retired to Nun Appleton in Yorkshire. Following Cromwell's death in 1658, Fairfax came out of retirement and was instrumental in the Restoration of Charles II.

up the east tower, fragments of which still lie within the inner ditch. The curtain wall, gates and towers were also partially destroyed, but the mansion constructed by Edward Manners was preserved.

The castle, manor and borough of Helmsley, the advowson of the church and other associated manors were granted to Fairfax and his heirs in 1650. Seven years later, George Villiers, the second Duke of Buckingham, who had fled the country following Charles I's defeat, recovered his familial estates through

his marriage to Fairfax's only daughter, Mary. George rapidly regained his social standing following Cromwell's death, becoming a member of the Privy Council and Lord Lieutenant of Yorkshire. The duke was notorious throughout England as one of the most profligate of Charles II's courtiers. The duke's pursuit of pleasure resulted in four episodes of imprisonment in the Tower of London. George retired to Helmsley in 1685 in ill health and poor finance, and died in 1687 after catching a chill while out hunting.

THE 18TH AND 19TH CENTURIES

George left no heirs and, in 1689, an act was passed allowing the trustees to sell his estates, including Helmsley, to settle his outstanding debts. In 1695, Helmsley was sold to Charles Duncombe, a London banker and later Mayor of London, for £90,000. Following his death in 1711, Helmsley passed to Thomas Browne, Duncombe's

brother-in-law and business partner. Browne took the Duncombe name and lived in Yorkshire, but he found the Tudor mansion at Helmsley to be an unsuitable residence and began building Duncombe Park. This Baroque country house was designed by William Wakefield of Huby Hall, possibly with advice from Sir John Vanbrugh, and is set within the former parks of the medieval castle and the lands of Rievaulx Abbey.

DUNCOMBE PARK

Above: Rievaulx Abbey provided the backdrop to the 18th-century Rievaulx terrace and temple

Left: A portrait, by John Riley, of Charles Duncombe, who bought Helmsley Castle in 1695

THE SECOND DUKE OF
❖ BUCKINGHAM ❖

George Villiers, the second Duke of Buckingham, was notorious for his extravagant and disreputable lifestyle. Following his father's death, George was raised with the children of Charles I, and was exiled during the Civil War for his loyalty to the Crown, returning only to be imprisoned in 1657. On his release, he married Mary Fairfax, the only heir of Thomas Fairfax, thereby regaining the rights to his title and familial property. George also regained royal favour after the Restoration, becoming one of the principal members of government as Lord Lieutenant of the West Riding. However, he was as well known for his private life as

NATIONAL PORTRAIT GALLERY, LONDON

A portrait of the second Duke of Buckingham, by Sir Peter Lely, c.1675

his public life. A notorious philanderer, George had affairs with many of the ladies at Court, most notably with the countess of Shrewsbury. This culminated in a duel between George and the earl of Shrewsbury, in which the earl was killed. George's reputation was badly damaged by this episode and his political standing declined. He spent his remaining years between Helmsley Castle and York, in poor health and in poverty. He died in 1687, after catching a chill while out hunting. He is immortalized in Dryden's allegorical poem *Absalom and Achitophel*, and in the children's rhyme: 'Georgie Porgie Pudding and Pie, kissed the girls and made them cry.'

The remains of Roche Abbey were reworked in 1774 by Lancelot Capability Brown, to create a picturesque ruin within a newly Romanticised landscape

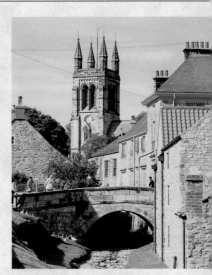

A watercolour of Helmsley Bridge, by James Bourne. The east tower can be seen just above the trees in the centre of the painting

Helmsley Castle provided a suitable Romantic backdrop to the vistas from the drive to Duncombe Park and the terrace temples. The use of ruins in such a way was also exploited at other sites in Yorkshire, such as Roche Abbey and Studley Royal. The walled garden, to the south-west of the castle, was established in 1758.

Helmsley Castle and Duncombe Park remained in the Duncombe family. Charles Duncombe was created Lord Feversham in 1826. His successor, William, employed

Helmsley was a place of some importance even before the foundation of the castle. All Saints' Church was established before the Norman Conquest, as was the former crossroads on which the town is located. The western arm of the crossroads has been lost, but it would have passed to the north of the current castle site, towards Rievaulx Bridge. The eastern arm of the crossroads follows the northern side of the Market Place and Bond Gate. The northern and southern arms are reflected in the route of Bridge Street.

If the pre-Conquest existence of Helmsley provided a suitable context for the establishment of the castle, it was the presence of the castle and the initiatives of the lord that stimulated the growth of Helmsley into a recognisable town. Fursan (Robert de Roos II) was particularly active

THE TOWN OF HELMSLEY

in developing the town, at the same time as rebuilding the castle. It is possible that he organised the arrangement of narrow plots on Bridge Street, which were rented by craftsmen and traders. He would also have been able to exploit the rental value of his mill, next to Helmsley Bridge, as the townspeople were required to use it.

By this period, the market space had become a well-defined area, stretching from All Saints' Church to the River Rye and from Bridge Street to the eastern side of the castle. The lord's control of this commercial area was reflected in the looming presence of the castle's east tower. From the later medieval period onwards, the market area was gradually built over, eventually leaving the current Market Place. The 14th-century heightening of the castle's east tower allowed the lord to maintain his symbolic 'presence' over the townspeople.

The wealth of the town in the later 12th century is reflected in Fursan's grant of borough status, giving commercial rights and privileges to the town. This enabled Helmsley's wealthier traders to sell and manage lands, and to hold regular markets with tolls for traders. By the 16th century, however, many industries were developing, which were not reliant on the castle. The lands around the town were rich in natural resources, such as timber, coal and clay, which were exploited by the residents of Helmsley. Cottage industries were established in the town, especially linen-weaving in the 18th century. Wills from the late 18th century show the population of Helmsley to have been dominated by small farmers; however,

there was also a growing number of weavers. Other cottage industries such as tanning, chandlering and iron production also developed. These changes may reflect the alterations to landholding practices that affected Helmsley in the mid-17th century. The process of land enclosure and the emergence of larger-scale landholders forced many small farmers to cease working their own land, replacing them with larger-scale landholders. Many of the small farmers had to find alternative work in towns or in the new enclosure farms.

By the 19th century, the lands around Helmsley were totally enclosed, creating a more efficient agricultural system and improving the market trade of the town. Living conditions in the town, however, were deteriorating, and in the mid-19th century, a substantial amount of rebuilding was undertaken by the second Lord Feversham, reusing a lot of masonry from the castle. Key improvements included the paving of the main streets, the provision of domestic gas in 1868 and the arrival of the railway in 1871. The gas works were located on the site of the present Visitor Centre.

Above left: All Saints' Church in Helmsley, seen from the Borough Beck
Below: The market place in Helmsley, with the castle's east tower in the background

was rebuilt by William Ernest Slingsby Duncombe using parts of the original design. The building remains in the Duncombe family and is still the residence of Lord Feversham.

THE 20TH CENTURY

By the early 20th century, the castle had ceased to be used as a quarry, but it was covered in ivy, rubble and earth. The area between the south-west range and the east tower had been levelled to make a lawn tennis court, and part of the site was occupied by a chicken run. The current appearance of Helmsley Castle owes much to Sir Charles Peers's work after the site passed into State guardianship in 1923. The castle was cleared of debris and the remains of buildings exposed and consolidated. The ditches were emptied of rubble, much of which had come from the demolition of the castle after the Civil War. The castle ramparts were reformed from the cleared material, according to the assumed original profile. Misleadingly, gaps in the rampart between the inner and outer ditch at the southern corner were

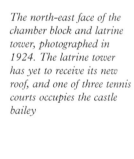

A 19th-century Romantic view of the snow-covered remains of the east tower, by Thomas Girtin

Charles Barry, the architect of the Houses of Parliament, for alterations to Duncombe Park in the mid-1840s. The building was devastated by fire in 1879 and a smaller fire in 1895 caused yet more damage, and so it

The north-east face of the chamber block and latrine tower, photographed in 1924. The latrine tower has yet to receive its new roof, and one of three tennis courts occupies the castle bailey

ENGLISH HERITAGE/NMR

ENGLISH HERITAGE/NMR

GETTY IMAGES/HULTON

filled in. The latrine tower received a new roof and the chamber block was repaired.

Nearly 300 years since it last saw active service, the castle had a military role during the Second World War. The castle's extensive and deep earthworks were ideal as an anti-tank measure and were used as part of a defensive network around Helmsley. Fortunately, the defences were not tested and the castle passed from the control of the Ministry of Works to English Heritage in 1984.

Above left: The east tower seen through the remains of the south gate. This photograph was taken just before the castle was cleared and consolidated

Above right: The interior of the chamber block undergoing repairs in the 1920s

The castle seen from the walled garden at Duncombe Park, which was established in 1758, after its predecessor, near the River Rye, was washed away by a flood

JOHN GOODALL

PLAN OF HELMSLEY CASTLE

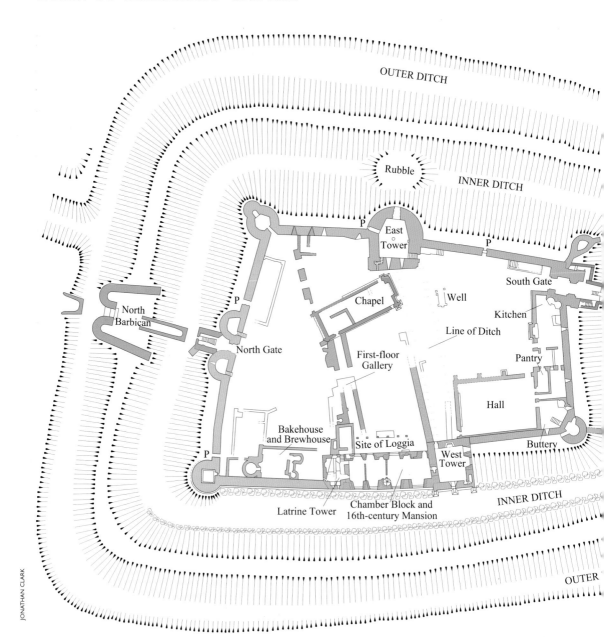

OUTER DITCH

INNER DITCH

Rubble

North
Barbican

North Gate

East
Tower

P

P

South Gate

Chapel

Well

Kitchen

Line of Ditch

First-floor
Gallery

Pantry

Hall

Bakehouse
and Brewhouse

Site of Loggia

West
Tower

Buttery

Latrine Tower

Chamber Block and
16th-century Mansion

INNER DITCH

OUTER

JONATHAN CLARK